LEARN COMPUTING

What If?

Anne Rooney

QEB Publishing

Library of Congress Control Number 2004101527

ISBN 1-59566-041-0

Written by Anne Rooney
Consultant Philip Stubbs
Designed by Jacqueline Palmer
Editor Anna Claybourne
Illustrator John Haslam
Photographer Ray Moller
Models supplied by Scallywags

Screenshot credits
Page 18 top /Zoo Tycoon, Marine Mania, Microsoft
Corporation /bottom Dogz 4, PF Magic, Ubisoft;
page 22 the Met Office.

Creative Director Louise Morley
Editorial Manager Jean Coppendale

Printed and bound in China

The words in **bold** are
explained in the Glossary
on page 31.

Contents

What's it about?

You've probably made models since you were small, using plastic bricks, cardboard, or modeling clay. A model shows us what something looks like and how it works or behaves.

Computer models

You can also make **models** of a different kind on a computer. Computer models are useful in many areas of life. For example, architects, engineers, and designers experiment with models, trying out different designs for buildings, bridges, vehicles, and machines.

Simulations

A **simulation** is a model of a process, such as a journey or an event. Computer simulations are used to plan trips by spacecraft, to teach pilots how to fly planes, and to practice or experiment with dangerous or expensive activities.

Spreadsheets

Governments and businesses use computers to model and plan spending and changes in society. Many of these models are made using spreadsheets—computer programs for working with numbers.

Find out how much money you can raise from a sponsored skate-boarding day.

You can use computers to make models, too. In this book, you'll find out how to use spreadsheets to model different situations, and see what happens when you change the numbers.

Find out how much paint you will need to buy to redecorate your room.

You'll also find out how to make a computer model do math for you, how to put your results into a graph, and even how simulations and spreadsheets can help forecast the future.

How does it work?

Spreadsheets are computer documents used for working with numbers. They let you make lots of calculations easily, and update all the answers immediately if you make any changes. They let you see how things would be if you changed any part of your plan.

Rows of cells

A spreadsheet has rows of **cells**. Each cell on a spreadsheet is a rectangle in a grid. A cell can hold a number, some words, or an instruction to do a calculation. An empty spreadsheet looks something like this:

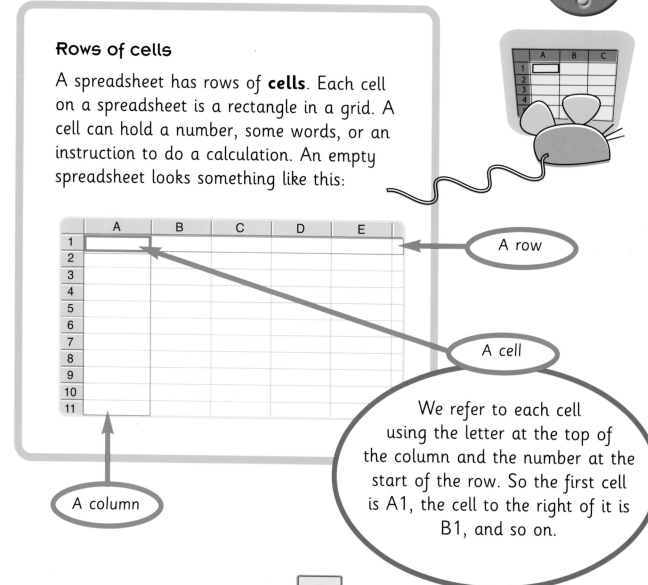

A row

A cell

A column

We refer to each cell using the letter at the top of the column and the number at the start of the row. So the first cell is A1, the cell to the right of it is B1, and so on.

When it's being used, a spreadsheet looks like this:

	A	B	C	D	E
1	**Allowance money modeler**				
2					
3	Alex gets		$ 5.00		
4	Jenny gets		$ 8.00		
5					
6	A remote controlled car costs				
7	$ 40.00				
8					
9	It will take Alex		8	weeks to save	
10	It will take Jenny		5	weeks to save	
11					

Plan your spending

This spreadsheet is a model of how someone might spend $10 of birthday money. It lists three items and their prices. The spreadsheet adds up the prices to give a total in a separate cell.

	A	B	C
1	**Birthday money**		
2			
3	Pencil case	$5.50	
4	Gel pens	$4.50	
5	Trading cards	$3.50	
6			
7	**Total**	**$13.50**	
8			

Making changes

Spreadsheets are useful because you can change the numbers and see different results. For example, if you changed the second item from pens to a notebook, the computer would work out the sum total again:

	A	B	C
1	**Birthday money**		
2			
3	Pencil case	$5.50	
4	Notebook	$3.99	
5	Trading cards	$3.50	
6			
7	**Total**	**$12.99**	
8			

Make your own spreadsheet

The easiest way to see how a spreadsheet works is to make your own. Here's how to make a simple one about you and your friends' heights.

Words and numbers

Using your spreadsheet software, start a new spreadsheet and click in the first cell. Type in the title:

How tall are we?

In the cells underneath, type a list of your friends' names. In the cell to the right of each name, put each person's height in inches (you can guess if you don't know).

	A	B	C
1	**How tall are we?**		
2			
3	Ally	49	
4	Luke	48	
5	Alex	53	
6	Sara	52	
7	Max	54	
8	Paige	51	
9			

	A	B	C
1	**How long are we?**		
2			
3	Ally	49	
4	Luke	48	
5	Alex	53	
6	Sara	52	
7	Max	54	
8	Paige	51	
9		307	
10			

Adding up

So far, you've added text and numbers to the spreadsheet. Now it's time to make it do some work.

Click in cell B9, under the list of heights. Now type

=b3+b4+b5+b6+b7+b8

and press the Enter key.

This tells the spreadsheet to add up the numbers in cells B3–B8. It should change to show how long all of you would be, laid end to end.

If you want to check it, you can lie down with your friends and ask someone to measure you!

Using symbols

You tell a spreadsheet what to do using simple math symbols called **operators**. In a spreadsheet, this kind of instruction is called a **formula**.

The equals sign =

tells the computer it has to work out the answer and show it in the cell.

The formula we just used ...

=b3+b4+b5+b6+b7+b8

... tells the spreadsheet to do a sum total by adding the numbers in cells B3, B4, B5, B6, B7, and B8.

Another way to write this formula is

=sum(b3:b8)

This means "add up all the numbers (find the 'sum' of the numbers) in cells B3 to B8."

Working with data

The raw facts and figures that you put into a spreadsheet are called data. What you get out of a spreadsheet is information.

Yum yum!

Where does data come from?

The data you put into a spreadsheet usually comes from the world around you. It might come from a survey, such as asking your friends how many pets they have. Or you could collect data by doing an experiment—for example, by measuring people's heights, the temperature outside, or recording the growth of your pet rabbit.

To get the right information out of a spreadsheet, the data you put in needs to be accurate (correct), and you need to make sure you use the right formulas.

Seed experiment

Imagine you're growing two trays of alfalfa sprouts in two ways. You water one tray every day and the other every three days. Each day, you count how many seeds have sprouted. These measurements are your data.

You can tell just from this data that the seeds in tray 2 didn't grow as well. But by putting the data into a spreadsheet and making it do some sums, you can find out some more useful information:

Tray 1

2 4 9 14 17 17 18

Tray 2

0 2 4 6 7 7 6

	A	B	C	D	E	F	G	H
1		Day 1	Day 2	Day 3	Day 4	Day 5	Day 6	Day 7
2	**Tray 1**	2	4	9	14	17	17	18
3	**Tray 2**	0	2	4	6	7	7	6
4								
5	**Difference**	2	2	5	8	10	10	12

By subtracting tray 2's numbers from tray 1's numbers, the spreadsheet can show the difference between the trays.

DO IT!

To find the difference between the trays, the formula for cell B5 is:

On day 1: **=B2-B3**

On day 2: **=C2-C3**

and so on.

Remember to start each formula with an equal sign.

Other symbols are:

* for "multiply" **/** for "divide"

Sorting and ordering

A big spreadsheet can have lots of data in it. It's often easier to see patterns and find out facts if the data is listed in a particular order. Luckily, a spreadsheet can arrange your data in any order you like.

Paper problems

Imagine you had listed the heights of a group of people on paper. Maybe you wrote them down in the order in which you measured the people. So if you wanted to find the tallest person, you'd have to check every number on the list. That's easy with a short list—but what if you had listed everyone in your school?

How tall are we?

	122
Luki	124
Kate	129
Helena	131
Sarah	135
Alex	136
Max	

How tall are we?

Alex	
Helena	135
Kate	129
Luki	124
Max	122
Sarah	136
	131

If you wanted to put the list on the bulletin board in alphabetical order of name, or in order of height, you'd need to copy it all out again.

All in order

A spreadsheet can **sort** your data in any order you like at the click of a button. So you could put your friends in order of increasing or decreasing height, or in alphabetical order of name. And you can change the list around as many times as you like without having to do any more work!

	A	B	C
1	**Our ancestors**		
2		**Grade 4**	
3	U.K.	3	
4	N. America	4	
5	Africa	5	
6	Italy	7	
7	Sweden	6	
8			
9			

	A	B	C
1	**Longest rivers**		
2		**Miles**	
3	Nile	4,168	
4	Amazon	4,002	
5	Chang Jiang	3,986	
6	Huang He	3,414	
7	Ob-Irtysh	3,382	
8	Amur	2,760	
9			

	A	B	C
1	**Favorite drinks**		
2		**Votes**	
3	Cola	10	
4	Lemonade	7	
5	Fruit juice	6	
6	Milkshake	4	
7	Water	3	
8	Cocoa	1	
9			

DO IT!

Look for an option to "Sort" or "Order" your data. Pick the column or row you want to use for sorting—such as names or heights. You can also choose whether to sort in ascending order (0–9 or a–z) or descending order (9–0 or z–a).

Graphs and charts

It's often even easier to see what's going on, and to check your data is correct, if you can see it in the form of a graph or chart. Spreadsheets can do this for you, too.

Bar charts

A **bar chart** is a good way of showing numbers in different categories. This bar chart shows how many birds Luca saw in his garden between 8:00 and 8:30 every day for a week.

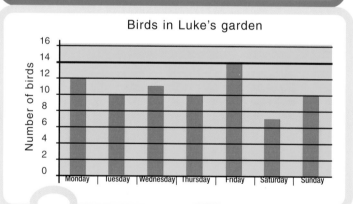

Bars, pies, and lines

There are several types of graph or chart. You need to pick one that suits what you're doing.

Sometimes a chart can help you see mistakes in your data. You might need to check your readings, or make sure that you copied the data into the spreadsheet accurately.

Pie charts

If you want to show proportions, a **pie chart** is best. This pie chart shows how children travel to school. It's easy to see at a glance how the class is divided.

Bus
10%

Car
27%

Bike
40%

Walk
23%

Pictograms

You can also use a **pictogram**. This shows piles of the things you are counting, such as how many ice-cream cones you're allowed per week:

Ice-cream cones per week

Luke | Lauren | Paige | Dionne | Ben | Danny | Jesse

Line graphs

A **line graph** is best if you have data based on occasional readings. For example, if you weighed a puppy once a week over three months, you could show the results as a line graph. Although the puppy grows all the time, you don't measure it all the time. The line fills in the gaps.

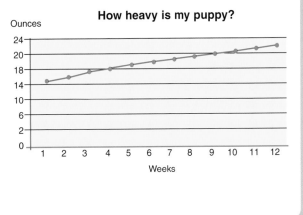

How heavy is my puppy?

Ounces

24
20
18
14
10
6
2
0

1 2 3 4 5 6 7 8 9 10 11 12

Weeks

Filtered facts

It's often useful to be able to pick out only some of the information in your spreadsheet. This is called filtering your data.

In the sun

Here's an example of how you **filter** useful data. This spreadsheet shows how many hours of sunshine you can expect each day in different beach resorts during the summer.

	A	B	C	D	E	F
1	Pick a vacation					
2					Hours of sunshine in	
3	Resort code	Place	June	July	August	September
4						
5	AB01	California	12	12	11	11
6	AB02	Bermuda	9.5	9.5	10	9.5
7	AB03	Mexico	9	10.5	11	10
8	EC01	California	10	12	12	11
9	EC02	Hawaii	8	9	10	8.5
10	EC03	Jamaica	11	11.5	11.5	11
11	RG04	California	10	11	11	10.5
12	RG06	Virgin Isl.	8	9	10	9
13	EW03	Antigua	9	9	9	8.5
14	EW06	California	9	10.5	11	10
15	NU12	Mexico	8	9.5	10.5	10
16	NU14	Florida	8	9.5	9.5	9
17	ZX02	California	10	11.5	11	10
18	ZX03	Florida	9.5	9.5	10	9

Where?

If you'd decided to go to California, you could ask the spreadsheet to show you only the information for California.

	A	B	C	D	E	F
1	Pick a vacation					
2					Hours of sunshine in	
3	Resort code	Place	June	July	August	September
4						
5	AB01	California	12	12	11	11
11	RG04	California	10	11	11	10.5
14	EW06	California	9	10.5	11	10
17	ZX02	California	10	11.5	11	10

When?

Or, if you were planning a vacation in August, you could ask your spreadsheet to show you only resorts that would have more than eight hours of sunshine a day in August.

	A	B	C	D	E	F
1	Pick a vacation					
2					Hours of sunshine in	
3	Resort code	Place	June	July	August	September
4						
5	AB01	California	12	12	11	11
7	AB03	Mexico	9	10.5	11	10
8	EC01	California	10	12	12	11
9	EC02	Hawaii	8	9	10	8.5
10	EC03	Jamaica	11	11.5	11.5	11
11	RG04	California	10	11	11	10.5
14	EW06	California	9	10.5	11	10
15	NU12	Mexico	8	9.5	10.5	10
17	ZX02	California	10	11.5	11	10
18	ZX03	Florida	9.5	9.5	10	9

Making filters

To filter data, you pick the column or row you want to use, then tell the spreadsheet what to look for. You can ask for exact matches or a range of data.

You need to use **operators** to tell the spreadsheet the range of numbers you want to look for. If you chose the "August" column, for example, you could then use these operators to filter the data:

equals =

=10

will find all resorts that expect exactly ten hours of sunshine

more than >

>10

will find resorts with more than ten hours of sunshine

less than <

<10

will find resorts with less than ten hours of sunshine

DO IT!

Look for an option to "Filter" your spreadsheet. You might be able to choose more than one thing to look for—for example:

Place = California AND August =>10

would look for resorts in California that had ten or more hours of sunshine a day in August.

Simulations

A simulation is a model of a real-life event or process. You might have played computer games that are simulations.

Types of simulations

There are lots of different kinds of simulation games—driving, flying a spaceship, keeping pets, building empires...

A simulation game could let you build and manage an imaginary zoo...

Or keep just one little virtual pet.

A simulation isn't as complicated as real life, but it can still be a very useful place to practice.

Imaginary worlds

Simulations aren't just for fun. They can be used to teach people real, important skills. For example, people learning to fly planes start by learning with simulators, so they can make mistakes safely.

Spreadsheets for modeling

The type of models in a simulation game are very complicated. Much simpler simulation models can be made with numbers in a spreadsheet.

Governments and organizations use spreadsheet models to work out complicated things, like how much money to spend on schools, or how to evacuate people in an emergency. They break down problems into lots of sum totals, and see how the results change when different things happen.

Working with money

A budget is the money available for a project. Your school has a budget—a fixed amount it can spend on books, teachers, sports equipment, etc.

Budget model

If you are planning a party and have a budget, you can use a spreadsheet to show how you could spend the money in different ways. This spreadsheet shows how many guests you could have with a $150 budget and two possible menus.

	A	B	C	D	E
1	Party planner				
2					
3	Menu A (per person)			Menu B (per person)	
4	Pizza	$ 3.50		Chili	$ 4.00
5	Chips	$ 1.00		Rice	$ 1.50
6	Ice-cream	$ 2.00		Tortillas	$ 1.00
7	Juice	$ 1.50		Salsa	$ 2.50
8				Juice	$ 1.20
9		$ 8.00			$ 10.20
10					
11	Budget	$ 150			
12					
13	Number of people				
14					
15	Menu A		18.75		
16	Menu B		14.70		

All change!

One of the main reasons computer models are so useful is that you can make changes and see how things would work out in real life.

Planning and design

Designers and other professionals often use models to test their plans. For example, an engineer designing a bridge will use a computer model to see what would happen if heavy traffic crossed the bridge, or if a hurricane hit it.

Using simulations

If you play a simulation game, or if there is a simulation program you can use at school, you can make choices and see what happens as you do different things. For example, a skateboarding simulation game will show you what happens if you skateboard too fast —sooner or later, you'll fall off!

Planning

People use spreadsheet models to help them make decisions and plan. Imagine a toy company has decided to make a new range of plastic monsters. They know how many monsters they can sell at different prices, so they use a spreadsheet to find out how much money they'd make at each price:

They sell more monsters if they're cheaper—so the model tells them they'll make the most money by selling their monsters at $5.99.

$5.99

	A	B	C	D	E
1	Price		Number of sales		Total
2	$5.99		700,000	monsters	$4,193,000
3	$6.99		500,000	monsters	$3,495,000
4	$7.99		400,000	monsters	$3,196,000
5					

Change your party plans

On page 19, you can see how to make a spreadsheet for a party budget. But what if you managed to make or buy a cheaper chili for your party? You could change the cost of chili and the spreadsheet would do the sums again.

	A	B	C	D	E
1	Party planner				
2					
3	Menu A (per person)			Menu B (per person)	
4	Pizza	$ 3.50		Chili	$ 3.20
5	Chips	$ 1.00		Rice	$ 1.50
6	Ice-cream	$ 2.00		Tortillas	$ 1.00
7	Juice	$ 1.50		Salsa	$ 2.50
8				Juice	$ 1.20
9		$ 8.00			$ 9.40
10					
11	Budget	$ 150			
12					
13	Number of people				
14					
15	Menu A		18.75		
16	Menu B		16		

How many people?

Or you could find out how much it would cost to have different numbers of people, using each menu:

	A	B	C	D	E
1	Party planner				
2					
3	Menu A (per person)			Menu B (per person)	
4	Pizza	$ 3.50		Chili	$ 4.00
5	Chips	$ 1.00		Rice	$ 1.50
6	Ice-cream	$ 2.00		Tortillas	$ 1.00
7	Juice	$ 1.50		Salsa	$ 2.50
8				Juice	$ 1.20
9		$ 8.00			$ 10.20
10					
11	Budget	$ 150			
12					
13	Number of people				
14		Menu A		Menu B	
15	5	$ 40.00		$ 51.00	
16	10	$ 80.00		$ 102.00	
17	15	$ 120.00		$ 153.00	
18	20	$ 160.00		$ 204.00	
19	25	$ 200.00		$ 255.00	

Finding patterns

If there's a pattern or trend in a set of data, models can help us work out what's likely to happen next.

Weather modeling

Weather forecasts are an example of using models to predict what's going to happen. Meteorologists (people who study weather) keep records of the weather and look for patterns. These patterns are used to make computer models that can work out what the weather's likely to do next.

SATURDAY

	A	B
1	Times tables	
2		
3	1	9
4	2	18
5	3	27
6	4	36
7	5	45
8	6	54
9	7	63
10	8	72
11	9	81
12	10	90
13	11	99
14	12	108

Number patterns

You can use a spreadsheet to see patterns in numbers, too. This spreadsheet shows the nine times table, up to 12 x 9.

You can see that in each of the numbers to 12—8, 27, 36, etc.—the digits add up to nine:

18	1 + 8	= 9
27	2 + 7	= 9
36	3 + 6	= 9

But does that always happen?

With a spreadsheet, it's easy to check. You can continue the spreadsheet up to any number you like. You'll find that from 21 x 9, the digits sometimes add up to 18 instead.

 DO IT!

To make the nine times table spreadsheet, you need to put numbers counting upward from 1 in column A. Then in cell B3 put the formula:

=a3*9

You can then use an option to "Copy" or "Replicate" this cell down the column. When you copy it, the spreadsheet changes the formula so that it's right in each row. So in cell B6, the formula will be:

=a6*9

If you wanted the spreadsheet to show the eight times table instead, you'd change the formula in B3 to:

=a3*8

and copy this into all the cells in the column.

Perfect!

If you use a spreadsheet in a project or to present the results of an experiment, make sure it's clear and easy for other people to understand.

Nice and clear

When you first make a spreadsheet, what you're doing is fresh in your mind, so you might not think you need to label the cells. But later, when you've done some other work, you could forget what your spreadsheet actually shows.

A spreadsheet like this, that's just numbers with no titles or labels, won't mean much to you—and it sure won't make sense to anyone else!

	A	B	C
1	June 03		3
2	June 10		2
3	June 17		0
4	June 24		1

So remember to add clear, accurate labels like these when you make a spreadsheet.

	A	B	C	D
1	Basketball scores			
2				
3	Match date		Points we scored	
4	June 03		3	
5	June 10		2	
6	June 17		0	
7	June 24		1	

Is it right?

As long as you put the right data into a spreadsheet and give it the right instructions, it will give you the right answers. But if you make a mistake, it will go wrong. Always do a few rough calculations to make sure the answers in your spreadsheet make sense.

Here are some of the reasons a spreadsheet can go wrong:

- You've used the wrong formulas.

- You've made a mistake putting your data into the spreadsheet, like putting numbers in the wrong order or missing something out. (Remember, making a graph can help you see mistakes like this.)

- You've mixed up different units (putting some lengths in yards and some in inches, for example).

Always check your work carefully when you put your data in, and when you look at the answers.

Projects to try

Now it's time to put your spreadsheet skills into practice. Here are some fun projects to try out yourself.

Leg counter

How many legs are there in your backyard? There are hundreds of minibeasts in a lawn, and lots of them have legs. You can't count all of them, but you can count a sample and use a spreadsheet to help you estimate how many there are in total!

Don't have a yard at home? You could try this experiment in a school or sports ground instead.

Start by measuring out a one yard square area of your backyard, and counting all the minibeasts you can find in it. Make a recording sheet so you can check them off as you find them:

Spiders   ///
Beetles   //
Centipedes   //
Worms   ////
Slugs   //
Flies   ///

Start your spreadsheet

On the computer, open up your spreadsheet program, and start a new spreadsheet. Put in the data in the form of labels and numbers, like this:

You'll need to put a formula in the cells in the "Total legs" column to work out the total number of legs for each type of minibeast.

	A	B	C	D	E
1	Minibeast leg counter				
2					
3		Number found		Legs each	Total legs
4	Spiders	5		8	
5	Beetles	6		6	
6	Centipedes	1		30	
7	Worms	4		0	
8	Slugs	1		0	
9	Flies	2		6	
10	Woodlice	3		14	

For example, if the number of beetles you found is in cell B5, and the number of legs a beetle has is in D5, the formula you need in E5 is:

=B5*D5

How many legs in all?

At the bottom of the "Total legs" column, add up all the legs using the "sum:" formula.

A backyard full of legs

Now find out the total for your whole backyard. If you counted minibeasts in one square yard and your whole lawn is 70 square yards, you need to multiply your total by 70:

	A	B	C	D	E
1	Minibeast leg counter				Total
2					
3		Number found		Legs each	Total legs
4	Spiders	5		8	40
5	Beetles	6		6	36
6	Centipedes	1		30	30
7	Worms	4		0	0
8	Slugs	1		0	0
9	Flies	2		6	12
10	Woodlice	3		14	42
11	In one square yard:				**160**
12	In whole backyard:				11,200

In this case, the total goes in cell E12, using the formula:

=E11*70

More projects to try

Put it in a pie!

Find some information from history that you could show as proportions. Put the information into a spreadsheet and use it to make a pie chart. It works best if you choose simple data.

Henry's wives

Henry VIII of England had six wives, who met with various different fates:

Catherine of Aragon	–divorced
Anne Boleyn	–beheaded
Jane Seymour	–died
Anne of Cleves	–divorced
Catherine Howard	–beheaded
Catherine Parr	–survived

You could draw a pie chart like this from the data:

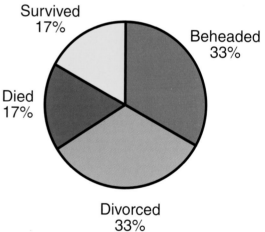

Survived 17%
Beheaded 33%
Died 17%
Divorced 33%

More ideas for pie charts

How much of your day do you spend eating, studying, relaxing, and asleep?

What do you spend your allowance money on?

What are the favorite colors of the people in your class?

How many fish?

For this project, see if you can find out how to make the spreadsheet, and what formulas to use.

Imagine you wanted to keep tropical fish. You can get tanks in these sizes:

20 x 30 x 20 inches
30 x 40 x 20 inches
30 x 60 x 20 inches

You can keep five fish in the smallest tank. Can you make a spreadsheet to find out how many fish you could keep in each of the other tanks?

	A	B	C	D	E	F	G	H
1	How many fish?							
2								
3	Sizes			Volume		Fish		Per Fish
4	20	30	20			5		
5	30	40	20					
6	30	60	20					
7								

Handy hint

Put the sizes of the sides in different cells, like this.

More tips

Use a formula to find out the volume of each tank, by multiplying the lengths of sides together.

Work out how much space each fish needs, by dividing the volume of the first tank by the number of fish (5).

Find out how many fish can go in each of the other tanks by dividing the volume of each tank by the volume needed for each fish.

Grown-up zone

What if?

This book will help a child to:

- Use a spreadsheet to process data from an experiment or survey.

- Spot and test mathematical patterns.

- Use a spreadsheet model to find optimum dimensions for a technology project.

- Use a spreadsheet to sort or filter data from a history or geography project and produce graphs.

Children should incorporate planning, drafting, checking, and reviewing their work in all projects they undertake. They should discuss with others how their work could be improved, whether information technology methods are the best choice for a given task, and how computer methods compare with manual methods. They should look at ways of combining information technology and manual methods of working.

Curriculum resources online

Education World: Technology in the Classroom:

www.educationworld.com/a_tech/

Educational Technology in the Federal Resources for Educational Excellence collection:

wdcrobcolp01.ed.gov/cfapps/free/displaysubject.cfm?sid=2

International Society for Technology in Education:

www.iste.org/resources/

Further resources

There is a large number of simulation games on the World Wide Web which you can use with children. Encourage children first to play the game and then to discuss:

- How the simulation is and is not like real life.

- The limitations of the simulation.

- What might happen if they carried out certain actions.

- How a similar simulation might be used for training, experimentation or some other application, other than play.

We advise that you look for and check simulation games yourself to make sure they are appropriate for your children.

Glossary

Bar chart

Chart in which the height of the columns (bars) shows the frequency or number of the thing being counted.

Cell

A single rectangle in the grid of a spreadsheet.

Filter

To extract a particular type or category of information from a spreadsheet or database.

Formula

Instruction used to make a spreadsheet do a sum total.

Line graph

Graph made by adding lines between plotted points.

Model

A pretend version of something real.

Operator

Special symbol or word used in a spreadsheet formula or filter.

Pictogram

A type of graph or chart that uses little pictures of the objects that are being counted.

Pie chart

Chart made by dividing up a circle to show proportions.

Simulation

Model of a process or situation used to try things out on a computer.

Sort

To arrange information into a particular order.

Index